YOU WERE BORN TO WIN

YOU WERE BORN TO WIN

ADVICE TO YOUTH ON LIVING WITH PURPOSE AND CREATING AN UNDEFEATABLE SELF

DAISAKU IKEDA

World Tribune Press

Published by World Tribune Press
A division of the SGI-USA
606 Wilshire Blvd.
Santa Monica, CA 90401

Printed in the United States of America.

Cover and interior design by Lightbourne, Inc.

21 20 19 18 2 3 4 5

ISBN: 978-1-944604-09-7

Library of Congress Control Number: 2017947774

CONTENTS

EDITOR'S NOTE

You Were Born to Win contains selected passages from a variety of Daisaku Ikeda's works on subjects of particular interest to young people. Though originally written for a specific audience at a specific time, the passages offer a universal message. The sources of the selections can be found in the References section at the end of the booklet.

These same selections appear as chapter seventeen of *The Wisdom for Creating Happiness and Peace, Part 2: Human Revolution*, published by World Tribune Press in 2017.

The citations most commonly used in this booklet have been abbreviated as follows:

LSOC, page number(s) refers to *The Lotus Sutra and Its Opening and Closing Sutras*, translated by Burton Watson (Tokyo: Soka Gakkai, 2009).

OTT, page number(s) refers to *The Record of the Orally Transmitted Teachings*, translated by Burton Watson (Tokyo: Soka Gakkai, 2004).

WND, page number(s) refers to *The Writings of Nichiren Daishonin*, vol. 1 (WND-1) (Tokyo: Soka Gakkai, 1999) and vol. 2 (WND-2) (Tokyo: Soka Gakkai: 2006).

INTRODUCTION

In an informal discussion with SGI President Ikeda, a youth division member from overseas said: "I made a fresh determination in faith six months ago, but none of my problems have been resolved yet and I don't feel as if anything has particularly changed in my life. It doesn't seem to make any real difference whether I practice or not." In response, President Ikeda offered the following advice:

> *It's important not to be impatient but to take the long view. It's very hard to tell how much a tree, for example, has grown in a month or half a year. But after twenty or thirty years, it will grow to an impressive size. We practice Nichiren Buddhism to create happiness in this lifetime and throughout eternity; it is all the more important, therefore, to have a long-term perspective in faith.*
>
> *Being a Buddha doesn't mean having no problems or worries. In fact, a Buddha invariably has lots of them. For a Buddha is always concerned and struggling with how to help all humanity become happy and create a peaceful world.*

So having lots of problems is a good thing; it's what enables you to become a Buddha. If all your problems were instantly solved after just a bit of chanting, your faith would never deepen and you wouldn't be able to really do your human revolution or change your karma.

The Gohonzon is giving you the opportunity to challenge yourself and grow. If you can look at your situation that way and chant with a spirit of appreciation, that will show that you are in fact progressing in your human revolution.

President Ikeda is a leader who loves young people and places immense trust in them, tirelessly encouraging them with compassionate concern. This booklet features some of his messages to youth.

COURAGE, CONVICTION, AND HOPE

President Ikeda stresses that the time of youth is important for building the foundation of our lives, and that courage, conviction, and hope are young people's great treasures.

Most people have many memories of their youth, and I am no exception. Those who don't cannot really be said to have lived their youth fully.

My family was poor, and my four older brothers were all drafted into the army and sent to the battlefield during World War II. I found a job to support my family. Financial and time constraints meant that I had to continue my high school and college education at night while working during the day.

My health was also not very good. But I was determined to devote myself wholeheartedly to my job. Sometimes, when making deliveries for the company I worked for, I had to pull a large cart around the fashionable Ginza area. I also had to get by with only a single dress shirt, even when the cold autumn wind started to blow. But I never felt the least bit of shame or embarrassment because of that. In fact, I saw my struggles as the dramatic adventures of a youth challenging hardships with a smile, and even regarded them as a source of pride. It is certainly true that all of those youthful efforts became the foundation for my life today.

At that time, I was convinced—or, should I say, determined—that I would not spend my youth in vain pursuits. I would make my way proudly in society, just as I was, developing my capabilities and living my life to the fullest. That determination, which sustained me in my youth, remains unchanged to this day. The greatest winners in life are those who ultimately triumph as human beings, irrespective of worldly position, wealth, and honor. I intend to remember this as long as I live.

But with the benefit of hindsight, there are some things I wish I could have done differently in my youth. For instance, I wish I could have acquired more in terms of my basic education in my teens and twenties. I also wish that I had done more to build up a strong and healthy body. And though I realized the importance of my youthful days and read quite a few books at the time, today I deeply regret not having read ten or twenty times as many.

Looking back at my own youth, I keenly appreciate how important this period of one's life is. It is no exaggeration to say that how we spend our youth largely determines the rest of our lives.

Young people are works in progress, not yet complete. That's what makes each young person an unknown quantity with limitless potential. Youth are a vibrant force for new, positive change; they are bursting with energy and vitality. Nothing is more wonderful than this.

I truly feel that courage, conviction, and hope are qualities vital for youth to possess. The courageous efforts of young people are a source of amazing creativity. And courage is supported by conviction. When we have conviction, we are free of hesitation or doubt. Conviction, in turn, is born of our efforts to fulfill our mission and responsibilities. The most outstanding individuals are those who hold fast to the ideals of their youth, to the dreams they had when they were young.

Young people are the treasures of a nation and the wealth of tomorrow's world. Nothing is more precious. Undermining the future of youth and robbing them of their vitality is like tossing that treasure into the sea. And leaders who tragically force young people to fight in wars, making them cast away their lives, are indeed the most reprehensible of villains.

I love young people. Nothing delights me more than their growth. I am thrilled when I see them developing into wise, peace-loving, and happy individuals. I also cherish the hope that I may walk alongside them and maintain a youthful spirit as long as I live.

My one and only wish, and my greatest happiness, is that a steady stream of young people will soar forth, from the foundations we have built, to work for world peace and create a flourishing of culture.

THE PROBLEMS OF YOUTH ARE THEMSELVES SOURCES OF LIGHT

With warm compassion and empathy, President Ikeda wholeheartedly encourages young people. He urges them to learn to encourage themselves, to like themselves, and to use their problems as fuel to shine ever more brightly.

Youth is a painful time. It is full of problems. But dealing with such troubles helps us grow as human beings. When we look back at the times we really suffered, the times we thought were the most miserable, we see that these were the most precious times of all.

That's why we need to grapple with our problems head-on, instead of trying to escape them. That is the most direct way forward.

If you're sad and lonely, then you should acknowledge those feelings. Don't try to distract yourself from them with shallow amusements. Don't diminish them. Go through those feelings, bravely weather them, and turn them into nourishment for your growth.

Somewhere in the World
a mission is waiting for you—
a mission only
YOU
can fulfill.

✡

People, just like flowers, need light. People's hearts wither when no one values or cares about them. So please be the sun that imparts bright light to all.

People, like flowers, also need water. Our hearts wither if we don't encourage ourselves, make ourselves happy, and spark our own enthusiasm.

Those who can encourage themselves are truly inspiring. They understand the pain and suffering of others. Find the words, strength, and wisdom to bring happiness to your own heart. When you're feeling down, lift up your own spirits.

If you can't like yourself, you can't love others.

✡

If you're shy and sensitive, that's perfectly fine. Being thick-skinned and insensitive is not a requirement for being an adult. Flowers aren't made of concrete, either; they are soft, delicate, and fragile. Those who remain sensitive to others' thoughts and feelings their whole lives are truly strong.

Our destiny does not come from somewhere outside us; it is shaped within our own hearts, day by day. If we find life boring, it might be because we've let ourselves become boring. If life seems empty, it might be because we've allowed ourselves to grow empty and shallow. If we feel fed up with life, then life might actually be saying the same to us! We can only lead lives that match the way we live them.

If you get average grades in school, that's fine, but please make sure you excel as a human being. Grades aren't the only measure of how smart or capable you are, and they really matter little in life over the long term. However, I hope you will earnestly pursue those questions that spark your curiosity and think long and hard about them.

Also, I hope you will become a person who is willing, at the crucial moment, to stand up for truth and justice, regardless of the personal cost. As the presence of such individuals grows, the world will become a more beautiful place.

Somewhere in the world a mission is waiting for you—a mission that only you can fulfill. It is waiting for you, counting the days. Since that is the case, you must live, you must keep going until the day you encounter your mission!

To shine, you must burn with an inner light, and the fire that produces that inner light is fueled by problems and suffering.

The problems of youth are themselves sources of light.

YOU ARE EACH A PRECIOUS INDIVIDUAL WITH A SPECIAL MISSION

President Ikeda stresses that we are all precious beings, each born with our own unique mission.

Everyone has a mission. We were born because we have a mission. That's why we must live our lives and persevere through all.

The Japanese word for mission means to "use one's life." For what purpose do we use our lives? For what purpose have we been born in this world, sent forth from the universe?

Buddhism views the universe as one giant life. If we compare it to a vast ocean, each individual life is like a wave on that ocean. When a wave rises from the ocean, that is "life"; when it merges back into the ocean, that is "death." In both life and death, each individual life is one with the universe.

The whole universe supports and assists in the birth of a single life. All of you have been sent here with the blessings and congratulations of the entire universe!

All life is equally precious. There is no hierarchy among living beings. Each being has a unique nature. Each person's life is as precious as the universe in its entirety—it is one with the universe and just as important.

Nichiren writes in this regard: "Life is the foremost of all treasures" (WND-1, 1125); "The Buddha says that life is something that cannot be purchased even for the price of an entire major world system" (WND-1, 983); and "One day of life is more valuable than all the treasures of the major world system" (WND-1, 955).

This is why we must never take our own lives, why violence, too, is wrong, and why we mustn't harm or bully others. None of us has the right to inflict harm on life, which is so precious.

Youth is a time when we ponder the meaning of our existence. It is like a "second birth." Our first birth is our physical birth. The second, our youth, is the time of our "birth" as human beings in the real sense. That's why it's painful. It requires the same kind of struggle and exertion as a chick breaking out of its shell.

The crucial thing is to never give up in that process. As you struggle and strive to find your way, please chant, think, study, talk with friends, and tackle the things you need to do now. If you continue to challenge yourself without giving up, you will come to see the mission that is yours and yours alone to accomplish.

SEEKING OUT CHALLENGES FOR SELF-DEVELOPMENT IN ONE'S YOUTH

President Ikeda explains that a springtime of exhilarating victory comes to those who remain true to their vow and convictions, actively seek out challenges, and develop themselves in their youth.

Only those who have experienced the harshness of winter can truly know the joy of spring. The same is true of life.

The Swiss philosopher Carl Hilty (1833–1909) asserted: "What joy is, is essentially known only to those who have suffered much. Others know only pleasure, which is in no way similar."[1] Those who haven't experienced suffering cannot know real joy—how true that is!

Hilty also wisely observed: "Happiness in life is not a matter of having few or no hardships but, rather, of victoriously and gloriously overcoming them all."[2]

True happiness in life lies in triumphing over every obstacle, he says. This point of view is quite similar to the Buddhist teaching that sufferings arising from earthly desires are the springboard to enlightenment.

There are some people who try to make their way through life without exerting any genuine effort, who try to profit and get ahead without putting in any hard work. Do they achieve real happiness? False veneers are eventually exposed, and pretense can only get one so far.

In the natural world, winter always turns to spring. What is needed in our human world for that to happen?

Hilty declared: "Break through!—this short phrase has an almost magical effect each time we face an inner crisis."[3] Persevere through all; continue, no matter what difficulty. Persevering is the secret to everything, he concludes.

To paraphrase Hilty: When your mind seems ready to drift off to sleep, or when you are overcome by a feeling of lethargy—tell yourself: "Break through!" This short phrase delivers a shock to a healthy will and awakens it. The elevated spirit is once again free to move toward the truth, toward what's right and just. When you feel yourself succumbing to feelings of futility or apathy, rouse yourself and press on through!

We all experience problems and deadlocks from time to time—it might be with SGI activities, with work, or with human relations. That's the time to persevere. Continue pressing forward and win your own victory. That's the only way.

There may be times when life itself seems a burden, when we feel trapped or weighed down by something, when we feel passive and a victim of circumstances, or when we feel somehow lost. Those are the times to shed our passivity and turn it into initiative, telling ourselves, "I'm going to follow through on this path!" "I'm going to carry out my mission for today!" When we decide to do so, a genuine spring will dawn in our hearts, and flowers will start to bloom.

Persevering for us means continuing in our efforts to chant Nam-myoho-renge-kyo and share Nichiren Buddhism with one person after another. We who know this sure and practical way for transforming winter into spring are fortunate indeed.

It is my fervent wish that a steady stream of outstanding SGI leaders for the twenty-first century will emerge from the youth division. Because of my strong hopes in that regard, I want to reiterate my advice that you continue to seek out challenges.

Mr. Toda often said: "Why did I become the president of the Soka Gakkai? It is because I lost my wife. I lost my beloved daughter. And because I have experienced all kinds of bitter hardships. That is the reason I became president." Because he had undergone great hardships, he was qualified to be president—this was Mr. Toda's philosophy.

Experiencing various hardships enables us to deepen our faith.

I still vividly recall the words of the Japanese industrialist [and founder of the Panasonic Corporation] Konosuke Matsushita (1894–1989), with whom I shared many conversations: "Mr. Ikeda, how true it is that people ought to struggle during their youth and even deliberately seek out hard work!"

These days, people try to avoid hard work. They seem to feel that working hard is old-fashioned or a waste of energy. However, this is certainly not the case. In essence, all of our efforts are for our own sake.

We live in an age in which people can easily indulge themselves as much as they like and leave everything up to others. Making efforts to train and develop oneself is not considered important. But such an attitude has caused many to lose their sense of purpose and identity.

Because of this prevailing climate, those resolved to actively seek out hard work will gain great reward and benefit. Those who thoroughly develop themselves and forge an undefeatable self will be victorious.

Where can we find such a wonderful realm of self-development? It is here in the SGI. Here, we find the path for securing supreme victory in life.

ALWAYS LOOK TO THE FUTURE

President Ikeda stresses the importance of living with a strong, positive, forward-looking spirit in one's youth, a time for building the foundations of one's life.

The German philosopher Friedrich Nietzsche (1844–1900) wrote: "Let where you are going, not where you come from, henceforth be your honour! Your will and your foot that desires to step out beyond you—let them be your new honour!"[4]

His message is that everything starts from now! Always look to the future! Buddhism also teaches the spirit of focusing on the present and the future. A meaningful life—and, in particular, a meaningful youth—is built not by focusing on the past, but on how you live from now on. That positive, forward-looking attitude is the key to greatness and victory. To continually apply yourself to the task of going beyond where you are today—that spirit of self-improvement is the very heart of youth.

President Toda urged young people to "strive constantly to improve themselves, to become more dignified and cultured, and to establish a better, greater self."[5] Develop yourself! This was his message to the youth. He also often encouraged them to read books and ponder things deeply.

You are the future leaders of society and kosen-rufu. That's why you need to think more deeply and strive more vigorously than those around you. Please take the initiative in working and studying hard. When you adopt that attitude, your eyes will sparkle and you'll enjoy a sense of fulfillment. If, on the other hand, you try to avoid hard work, you will lose your youthful freshness and vitality.

I continue to challenge myself, taking action and engaging in dialogue, with the spirit to put a week's worth, a month's worth, of effort into each day. I do it all for you, my fellow members, and for kosen-rufu. I never forget this guiding purpose.

Living without working to improve oneself leads to stagnation and, ultimately, self-defeat. There are those who fail to work on their own growth and development, using only their wits and wiles to get by. But the closing chapter of their lives is often empty and sad. They end up regretting the choices they made. They wish they could go back to their youth and do things differently.

There is a time for everything. If you have every material comfort and the freedom to do anything you please from the time of your youth, you are actually rather unfortunate. It's important that you forge inner strength and develop yourself in your youth. With such a foundation, it's only natural that once you reach a certain age your life will blossom, and you'll enjoy both spiritual and material rewards. This is the correct path in life.

KEEP MOVING FORWARD

Youth is another name for challenge.
Victory and success shine in tenacious efforts to
keep moving forward, undefeated by any obstacle.

Nothing is irredeemable in youth. The only real mistake you can make when you are young is giving up on yourself or allowing fear of failure to prevent you from trying to accomplish something.

The past is the past; the future is the future. Look to the future and keep moving forward, telling yourself: "Everything starts from today—it starts from now, this minute, this moment!" This is the essence of Nichiren Buddhism, the Buddhism of "true cause."[6] True success or failure in life will not be apparent until you reach your forties or fifties.

Don't allow your immediate situation to make you lose hope or panic. Though you may do something you regret, have problems, or make mistakes, the future is long. Don't be a fainthearted person who frets or despairs over every little thing.

When we look at the lives of famous people, we find that many had a far from perfect youth. For example, Sir Winston Churchill was well known for failing in school. Mahatma

> **The only real mistake you can make when you are young is giving up on yourself.**

Gandhi, too, was a mediocre student. He was shy, timid, and found it difficult to talk to others. Albert Einstein also didn't do well in some of his school subjects—though, of course, he was brilliant at mathematics. Wilhelm Röntgen, who discovered X-rays, was expelled from technical college because his classmates falsely accused him of something they themselves had done.

But what did all these individuals have in common in their youth? They never gave up on themselves. People who get poor grades, who are bullied, who are betrayed by their friends, who fail, who have to deal with such problems as illness or poverty, are more likely to understand others' feelings and have deep insights into life. The important thing, therefore, is not to be defeated. If you can do that, whatever suffering you have had to endure will definitely contribute in a positive way to your growth in the future.

You must love, respect, and treasure yourself. You'll be miserable if you allow yourself to be swayed by the prejudices, passing trends, and contradictions of society. Never forget to be who you are, to be true to yourself.

Mr. Toda sternly observed that the sense of happiness we feel in the final years of our life is what counts. It's got nothing to do with how well things go in your youth. Similarly, no matter how many times you fail at something when you're young, there's plenty of time to recover and get yourself back on course.

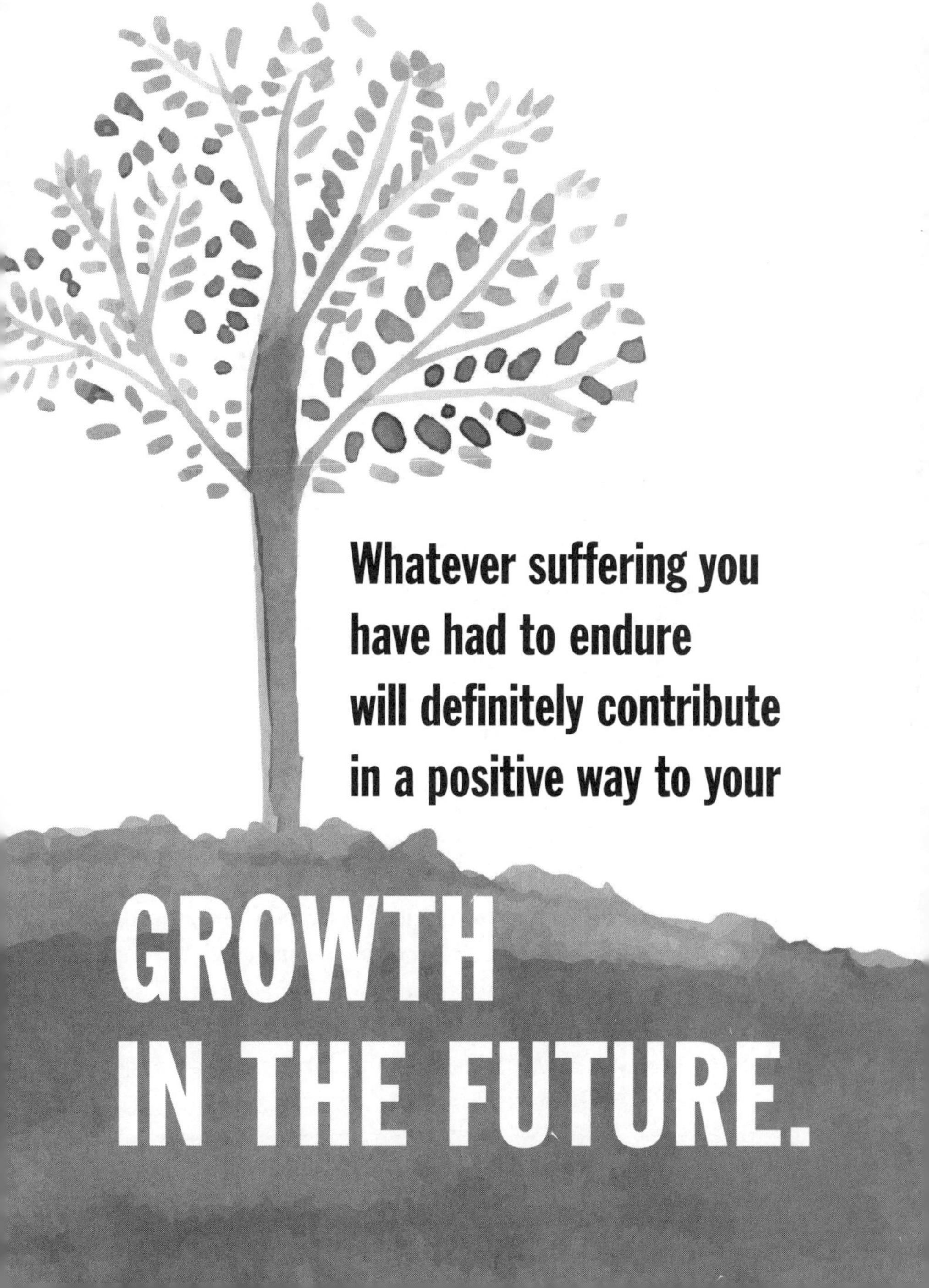
Whatever suffering you
have had to endure
will definitely contribute
in a positive way to your
GROWTH
IN THE FUTURE.

Never lose hope, never lose your aspiration to do better. If you don't do well in elementary school, there's always junior high. And if not in junior high school, then there is high school, college, and your entry into society after graduation. And if you experience setbacks along the way after that, continue challenging yourself into your forties, fifties, sixties, and seventies.

Moreover, from the profound perspective of Nichiren Buddhism, if you don't accomplish all you set out to in this lifetime, you can continue to fight on in the next lifetime and on for eternity. Faith in Nichiren Buddhism means cherishing the highest aspiration.

Even if you think you're hopeless and incapable, I know you're not. I have not the slightest doubt that each of you has a mission. No matter what others may say, I will always respect you and believe in you. No matter what your present situation is, I am absolutely certain that a wonderful future awaits you.

If you should fall, just get right back up. If you can pick yourself up, you can move forward. You are young. Now is the time for challenge and construction. Start from the present moment. Begin something, here and now.

✡

In every era, there is serious suffering. And in every era, youth is a time full of worries and emotional turmoil. School is not the only issue. There is family, health, looks, relationships, friends—all sorts of problems to deal with. There is suffering, anxiety, frustration, and sadness. Youth is a time of grappling with all sorts of problems.

Struggling for answers, dispelling dark clouds, and moving

Struggling for answers, dispelling dark clouds, and moving toward the sun, toward hope—this is the power of YOUTH.

toward the sun, toward hope—this is the power of youth. Of course, you will have problems, make mistakes, and have regrets. But what matters is not allowing them to defeat you. Just keep pressing forward, ever forward, pushing through all problems and suffering.

Suppose you are lost in the jungle. You want to find your way out and reach the ocean but don't know which way to go. What will you do? The answer is, keep moving ahead along any course until you come to a river. Then, if you follow the river downstream, you will eventually reach the ocean.

Move forward. As you struggle, chant Nam-myoho-renge-kyo and keep pressing ahead, even if only a millimeter, two millimeters. If you keep that up all your life, when you finally look back, you'll see you've made your way out of the jungle.

The more you suffer, the more sadness you experience, and the more you chant, the more profound a life you will lead. All will serve to nourish your growth into leaders of the twenty-first century.

LIVE WITH AN INVINCIBLE SPIRIT

Youth can be a time of emotional ups and downs, of being overly swayed by circumstances and feeling a sense of hopelessness and despair. For that reason, in this guidance for junior high school division members, President Ikeda stresses the importance of young people forging ahead with an invincible spirit.

Fortunate circumstances don't guarantee happiness, and, conversely, hard circumstances don't guarantee that one will be unhappy. Our environment doesn't decide our happiness; we do. We are either defeated by our environment or we triumph over it. That's what determines our happiness.

This doesn't just apply to school. There are many troubling, painful, unpleasant, and worrisome things in life. When you face such things, you have two options. You can complain, blame the environment, and be defeated. Some may express sympathy for you, but, ultimately, you're the one to lose out, and anything you say will really be just an excuse. The second option is to live with an invincible spirit, blazing your own way regardless of your environment. The choice is up to you.

In India, the caste system remains a deeply rooted social custom. It divides people into different social roles and ranks from birth. But there is someone who, though born into the lowest caste, rose to become president of India.

Our environment doesn't decide our happiness;

we do.

That is the current president (in 2000), Mr. K. R. Narayanan, with whom I have been friends for some time. Mr. Narayanan was the fourth of seven children. The family was destitute. Their home had no bath, and he was always hungry. Going to school each day meant walking four miles there and back. During the rainy season, the mud came up to his ankles. On those long walks, he was always reading. He couldn't afford to buy books, so he would eagerly read any newspapers or books he came across and take detailed notes.

Recognizing his love of study, Mr. Narayanan's elder siblings gave up their chance to go to elementary school so that he could get an education. But even then, the family often could not afford to pay his tuition. He was punished for this by being forced to stand outside the classroom, but he refused to let this get him down. He would simply strain to hear every word of instruction going on inside. Eventually, he was awarded a scholarship, one that had been established by Mahatma Gandhi, and was able to continue his studies. He graduated from university at the top of his class and became a diplomat. He recalls his youthful hardships with a smile. Because a diplomat had to be thick-skinned, he says, being forced to stand outside where all of his classmates could see him was good training.

He is a strong person. Strong people are happy. Happiness is found in a strong, resilient spirit.

It's possible for us to open a great path of hope so long as we don't succumb to the weakness of blaming others for everything that happens to us. We have to decide: "It's all up to me! I have to be strong." Complaining and making excuses is very unattractive. Blaming everything on your teachers, your parents, your friends—blaming others is not a very admirable way to live.

Napoleon Bonaparte declared that the environment was his to make. Decide never to blame your environment but instead to create the environment you desire.

I have always believed that, as young people with a mission, you cannot be defeated. Because you were born to win! Therefore, take aim at your dreams and strive your hardest to make them come true.

Even if you take a long, roundabout way to get there, what matters is that you succeed in crossing the finish line in the end. Become strong. Strong people are happy people.

Those who respond to painful circumstances by gritting their teeth and trying their hardest can obtain a rare and elusive treasure. In contrast, weak people, no matter how favorable their circumstances, will somehow turn those circumstances into a negative influence in their lives.

The way of life you choose determines your future. No one else makes the decision. No one else is to blame. It's entirely up to you, to how you live your life.

If you just let your environment control you, it becomes the main actor in your life. That is a regrettable way to live. You are the main actor, the one who determines the course of your own life.

TO YOUNG WOMEN'S DIVISION MEMBERS

President Ikeda offers important guidance for young women's division members with the wish that each one of them without exception will become genuinely happy.

In a letter to a woman, Nichiren writes: "Neither the pure land nor hell exists outside oneself; both lie only within one's own heart. Awakened to this, one is called a Buddha; deluded about it, one is called an ordinary person" (WND-1, 456).

Happiness and hell are within you, inside your own hearts and minds. Being a celebrity doesn't guarantee happiness. Neither does popularity. Honors and accolades are not true happiness, nor is wealth. The inner source of eternal, indestructible, absolute happiness is Nam-myoho-renge-kyo, which shines in the depths of your being. True happiness lies in tapping this source as you strive to cultivate your own life, which is still a work in progress. This is the essence of Buddhism.

The aim of our faith is for us to win in life. Buddhism is a set of principles to enable us to do so. To gloriously triumph in life, we need to strive just as always in our daily lives, carrying out our everyday responsibilities, and forge ahead with ever greater strength on the road of kosen-rufu.

When you do that, your life will shine with an endlessly noble spirit. The countless Buddhas of the ten directions and three existences will protect all of you—inspiring, unsung emissaries of the Buddha—as foremost champions of the world.

Don't allow yourself to be swept away by illusions. You cannot become happy by following people who are ignorant of the principles for genuine happiness. The absolutely correct way is to follow the Buddhism of Nichiren Daishonin, a true champion of humanity who left us the great pathway to happiness. Never forget that a wonderful luminous realm of eternal victory awaits those who embrace this teaching.

The course of your life is determined by whose lead you follow. Do you follow calculating politicians, vain pretenders, or greedy schemers? Do not be deceived. Your decisive choice must be to follow Nichiren Daishonin, the entity of the universe itself.

No matter what kind of father, mother, or siblings you may have, if you attain Buddhahood, you can lead all of them to enlightenment as well. The heart of Soka lies in building a happy, strong self.

Many labor under the delusion that marriage equals happiness. Remaining single by no means excludes you from enjoying happiness. The important thing is to build an unshakeable self, set on a foundation of correct faith. This is the way to true happiness.

Birds who don't fly lose the ability to do so. They lose the use of their wings and can't soar into the skies of happiness. An Olympic athlete who doesn't run or doesn't train cannot

Striving and progressing for some purpose or goal—this is the essence of

happiness.

win. Lazy people who don't strive, don't act, don't advance, end up losing in life.

Striving and progressing for some purpose or goal—this is the essence of happiness. If, from your youth, you strive tirelessly for the sake of others, for Buddhism, what an amazing person you will become! While carrying out your human revolution, you will build a truly expansive state of life.

As you may know, my wife, Kaneko, attended the inaugural meeting of the young women's division as a group leader (in 1951). With Tokyo as her main stage of activity from her youth, she has dedicated herself wholeheartedly to kosen-rufu.

Proud to be a Tokyo young women's division member [like all of you], she braved the cold winter winds during the historic February Campaign of Kamata Chapter (in 1952) to engage actively in sharing Nichiren Buddhism with friends and encouraging members.

Her parent's home was also a center for Soka Gakkai activities, so she invited her superiors at work to discussion meetings, helped make gatherings bright and enjoyable, and greeted with a smile the members who gathered there day and night. As a young women's division member, she would happily and kindly read picture books to children while their mothers attended the meetings.

Though no one was watching or praising her, she carried out the vow she made to President Makiguchi and worked to support President Toda. She assisted her mother, the chapter women's leader, encouraged her father, the district men's leader, and continued to strive for kosen-rufu with dedication, sincerity, and perseverance.

That exhilarating time as a young women's division member, my wife recalls, was the most memorable period of her life, when she built the foundation for her life and her Buddhist faith and practice.

Your fellow members around the world are all earnestly walking the path to absolute happiness. The Mystic Law, the great underlying principle of the universe! There is no other path to peace in the twenty-first century.

Let's advance along that path together! Social standing, wealth, position, and family background have nothing to do with happiness. And thinking you would be happy if things just went the way you wanted, or if you could just do this or that, is not really Buddhism.

"It is the heart that is important" (WND-1, 1000), Nichiren declares. The heart is faith, and faith is an essential requirement for happiness. The key is to become happy right here and now, in your present situation and circumstances, just as you are.

My young friends, be pioneers of life! Be great victors of happiness! Don't lose yourself in idle, empty, mundane pleasures and amusements! Take your place at the head of the march to fundamental happiness!

All of the heavenly deities as well as the Buddhas and bodhisattvas throughout the universe, radiant and dancing with joy, will protect your vibrant lives, shower you with the highest praises, and guide you on your journey to happiness.

TO APPRECIATE AND CARE FOR ONE'S PARENTS IS THE BASIS OF GENUINE HUMANITY

In a letter to his youthful disciple Nanjo Tokimitsu, Nichiren Daishonin writes, "A person who upholds the Lotus Sutra is repaying the debt of gratitude owed to father and mother" (WND-2, 638). Discussing this passage, President Ikeda teaches young people the importance of having appreciation for one's parents.

Once during an informal discussion with youth division members, Mr. Toda asked us who among Nichiren Daishonin's disciples we liked the most. I fondly recall replying without hesitation: "Nanjo Tokimitsu."

When Tokimitsu was only seven years old, his father, a man of great integrity, died of illness. The young boy met the Daishonin for the first time shortly thereafter, when the latter came to pray at his father's grave, an encounter that would stay with Tokimitsu forever. From that time on, he looked up to Nichiren as his teacher and, with his mother, strove earnestly in faith.

Tokimitsu studied and trained himself, growing into a fine

young man. When he was sixteen, he went to visit Nichiren who had moved to Mount Minobu. The Daishonin was no doubt delighted to see what an outstanding youth Tokimitsu had become. He sent him this letter, "The Four Virtues and the Four Debts of Gratitude," the following year (1275). In it, he instructs Tokimitsu that being a good son to the parents who raised him and repaying the debt of gratitude he owes them is the path of Buddhism.

The direct meaning of the passage "A person who upholds the Lotus Sutra is repaying the debt of gratitude owed to father and mother" is that upholding the Lotus Sutra is itself being good to one's parents. In other words, the Lotus Sutra has the power to repay the debt we owe them. This passage can also be read as a message to Tokimitsu that those who believe in the Mystic Law must not forget to appreciate their parents.

One passage of Mr. Toda's famous "Guidelines for Youth" reads:

> *Our struggle is one that requires that we develop compassion for all living beings. Yet there are so many young people who are incapable of having compassion for their own parents. How can they be expected to care about perfect strangers? The effort to overcome the coldness and indifference in our own lives and attain the same state of compassion as the Buddha is the essence of human revolution.*[7]

Love and gratitude for one's parents are the foundation of genuine humanity. Outstanding people invariably care for and treasure their parents. I have seen this through the friendships I have forged with leaders around the world.

Love

and gratitude for one's parents are the foundation of genuine humanity.

In his letter, Nichiren reminds Tokimitsu that his mother, when carrying him in her womb, must have undergone suffering that was close to death, while the pain she endured at the time of giving birth to him is almost too great to imagine (see WND-2, 637). Your mothers have undoubtedly endured terrible pain to give birth to you. Giving birth is truly a life-and-death struggle. On that point alone, we should feel and show gratitude to our mothers. That's why Mr. Toda was always very stern with those who didn't treat their parents well. He once thundered at a youth who made his parents worry: "Don't you know how much pain you're causing your parents!"

Immediately after the passage I have quoted, Nichiren writes, "Even if one does not feel in one's own heart that one can do so, one can repay it [the debt of gratitude owed to one's father and mother] through the power of this sutra" (WND-2, 638). What he means by these words is that the Mystic Law has the power to lead all people to happiness. By chanting deeply with faith in the Mystic Law and strongly living a good and correct life, we activate the positive functions of the universe and naturally develop a life state in which we can appreciate and treasure our parents.

The parents of many of you are exerting themselves earnestly as Soka Gakkai members, day after day, striving with tenacity and determination for the cause of the highest good. Together with me, they are dedicating their lives to realizing the supremely lofty mission of kosen-rufu.

Though they are working for the highest good, they may sometimes be unjustly scorned and criticized. Patiently enduring such bitter experiences, they are devoting themselves to the welfare of others, to Buddhism, and to society, pressing onward with unflagging fortitude. Their committed efforts make them more admirable than any celebrity or authority.

The Soka Gakkai was built by such great, yet unheralded, ordinary individuals. Steadfastly engaging one person after another in dialogue, they have built the Soka Gakkai into a remarkable global movement for peace, culture, and education.

They have also made such tireless efforts in order to open the way for your victory, motivated by their desire to bring good fortune and benefit to you, their beloved children. Though they may not say it in words, they are exerting themselves unsparingly for you, chanting, working, and striving as hard as they can. Such is a parent's love. You are deeply embraced and staunchly protected by your parents' prayers for your health, growth, and happiness. I hope that you will be proud to have such parents. I also hope that you will come to recognize their sincere dedication to their Buddhist practice and to the Soka Gakkai, and that you will become people of great wisdom and substance who respect and appreciate your parents from the bottom of your hearts, and who do your best to repay your debt of gratitude to them.

Perhaps some of you, like Tokimitsu, have lost one or both of your parents. But please remember that they live on in your hearts. When you chant Nam-myoho-renge-kyo to the Gohonzon, they are with you; they are always with you at the deepest level of life.

Perhaps some of you have parents who are not Soka Gakkai members, or with whom you have troubled or challenging relationships. In any case, please pray with open hearts for their happiness.

Stand up bravely on your own and live strongly based on faith. Triumph in your youth, and win boldly in life. Study hard, develop your minds and bodies, and become great leaders of kosen-rufu and society. Trying your hardest now, even if it's a struggle, is the very best way to repay your debt of gratitude to your parents. Such a sincere attitude will also make the spirit of mentor and disciple shine in your lives.

I hope that you will carry on the spirit of your parents, the Soka Gakkai, and the heritage of Soka mentors and disciples.

TRUSTWORTHINESS IS THE GREATEST ASSET FOR YOUTH

Reflecting on his own struggles in his youth, President Ikeda stresses how important it is for young people to gain others' trust and also to not be afraid of making mistakes.

Trust is an essential requirement for human life. For young people, in particular, trustworthiness is their greatest asset. A young person who fails to build trust is very unlikely to succeed.

Trust is difficult to build, yet easy to destroy. The trust one has worked hard to accumulate over a decade can be lost by a thoughtless word or action at a crucial moment. Carefully crafted facades tend to crumble at a critical juncture.

Those who persevere through hardships to carry out their own mission will ultimately win the trust of all around them.

I reserve the highest respect and admiration for those who, though having jobs that may be unexciting and out of the limelight, conscientiously apply themselves to their work, day in and day out, and patiently keep striving to improve themselves, one step at a time.

Though the trust of others is indeed precious, it can be ruinous for young people to adopt an overly cautious attitude, always playing it safe. The failures you experience at times in your youth can be incredibly valuable in building the foundation for your future. Young people should be aware of the fact that they are not perfect and should try to live each day with courage, true to themselves.

Those who lead resolute lives, who possess an invincible spirit and can rise up from the depths of despair like phoenixes from the ashes are much more likely to achieve brilliant victory in the end than those who have never experienced failure or disappointment. We should not be afraid of failure or mistakes but of letting them defeat us.

Allowing one or two setbacks to discourage us is foolish. Life is a long, long journey. However wonderful or successful our lives may seem along the way, if we end up suffering unhappiness and defeat in our final years, nothing could be more tragic. Please advance courageously with the conviction that the more mistakes you make in your youth, the more you can build the foundation for a new chapter in your life and for your lifelong happiness.

It's also important as young people to have the guts and integrity to honestly admit your errors. Never be so cowardly as to refuse to admit your mistakes and instead blame them on others. Being open-minded enough to calmly reflect and pinpoint where you went wrong can become the source of future value creation.

There is nothing more reassuring, refreshing, or beautiful than young people striving hard toward a goal. Nothing in all the world is more beautiful than the earnest struggles of youth.

Live
each day with
COURAGE
true to yourself.

OUR WORKPLACE IS AN IMPORTANT STAGE FOR OUR HUMAN REVOLUTION

President Ikeda offers warmhearted advice to young people about work based on his own experience and the guidance of second Soka Gakkai President Josei Toda.

Concerns about work can occupy a big place in the minds of young people. They may wonder what kind of work they are best suited for, or if their present job is the right one for them.

I had many of the same concerns when I was young. When I began working for Mr. Toda's publishing company, I started out as the editor of a boys' magazine. It was something I'd always wanted to do, but the company's business declined and the magazine was discontinued. I was then transferred to the kind of work I liked least, involved with finance. Additionally, there was a period when I didn't even receive my monthly salary. I couldn't buy an overcoat when winter came, but I never uttered a single word of complaint. My sole wish was to overcome the crisis facing Mr. Toda's businesses, and I worked single-mindedly toward that end.

Mr. Toda offered this advice to young people who were struggling with regard to their work:

> *There are three criteria for selecting a job—beauty, benefit, and good. Everyone's ideal is to get a job they like (beauty), that is financially secure (benefit), and where they can contribute to society (good). But the real world is not always that accommodating. Very few people find the job of their dreams from the very beginning. In most cases, we have to do work that we never expected we would do.*[8]

For example, our job may provide us a secure livelihood and contribute to society, but isn't something we enjoy or really suits us temperamentally. It provides benefit and good, but not beauty. Or we may have a job that we enjoy and contributes to society, but it may not provide us with enough money to support ourselves. It has beauty and good, but not benefit. Or our job may pay extremely well and be enjoyable, but have a negative effect on society. It has benefit and beauty, but not good.

As we can see, it can actually be quite difficult to attain all three values of beauty, benefit, and good. In the today's trying economic times, in particular, it is increasingly difficult to find a job at all.

What should we do then? Mr. Toda advised:

> *In times such as these, young people should not be discouraged. Just put all your energy into your present job and become an indispensable person there. By chanting earnestly to the Gohonzon and continuing to*

strive your hardest, not letting disagreeable tasks or assignments deter you, you will eventually find a job that you enjoy, offers financial security, and produces good for society. This is the benefit of faith.

And that's not all. When you look back at your less than satisfactory jobs, you'll find that none of your hard work was wasted; rather, you'll find it has all become a valuable asset for you. You'll come to understand that everything had meaning. I can assure you of this from my own experience. Our faith is expressed in our lives and in society. That is the power of Buddhism.[9]

Mr. Toda was a leader of unparalleled genius. I know from my own experience that what he says about work is true.

The important thing is to strive to win where you are now. Buddhism teaches that our lives are inherently and eternally endowed with Buddhahood and that this suffering-filled saha world is itself the Land of Eternally Tranquil Light (a wonderful realm where Buddhas dwell).

The important thing

IS TO STRIVE TO WIN

where you are now.

Therefore, shine where you are. By throwing yourselves into your work rather than avoiding it, you will definitely open a way forward in the best possible direction. Eventually, you will come to appreciate that all your efforts up to now had meaning, and everything you have experienced is a treasure for your lives. And when you do, you will be victors.

Young people who uphold the Mystic Law are happy. They will lead lives of satisfaction and fulfillment without fail.

I would like you to develop a life state where you can declare: "I am a truly fortunate youth. All my struggles are themselves sources of happiness." The true nature of such a person's life will reveal itself in their outward appearance and actions, in accord with the principle of the true aspect of all phenomena.

As long as you are lamenting your situation, looking gloomy and downcast, you'll be miserable and no one will recognize your abilities. You're far better off being upbeat and active. It will open the way to new possibilities. Your attitude determines everything.

I want each of you to be successful in your respective fields. You can't be a success if you make halfhearted efforts. You need to follow through on your chosen path to the very end. To do that, look at your job as your place of training where you build and develop yourself as a human being. This place of training as a human being is also your place of Buddhist practice, the place where you put your faith into practice. If you can adopt this outlook, all your complaints will disappear. Nothing is more pitiful than a person who is always complaining.

THOSE WHO ARE STRONG STAND ALONE

President Ikeda stresses that what is vital in youth is the courage to stand alone.

The German poet and playwright Friedrich von Schiller (1759–1805) declared that the strong are strongest when acting alone.[10] I have treasured these words since my youth.

It is not good to blindly follow the crowd. Going along with something without any real thought, just because everyone is doing it, or being quite content with not having to make any decisions yourself, leads to mental laziness and apathy. And that's dangerous. When everyone says that war is good, everyone rushes to war, without dissent or opposition, even if they know it spells disaster. No one has the courage to stand up and bravely declare: "War is wrong!" They just go along with the current social climate and whatever appears to be popular at the time.

But we mustn't be led astray. We must never abandon our commitment to peace, our desire to learn, and our love for humanity. Putting those values into practice ourselves and encouraging others to share them, too, takes courage.

Courage lies inside us. It is something we must rouse from within.

Mindlessly following the crowd is not courage but cowardice. It's fascism, not democracy. In a democracy, we each have to recognize that we are society's protagonists and as such have a responsibility to fulfill. Instead, there's too much self-interest—the attitude that "so long as I'm happy, that's all that matters"—and too much blind following—the mentality that "it's safer to go along with what everyone else says."

Only when people have the courage to stand alone can they lead the world in the direction of peace and good. When such courageous individuals join forces and unite in strong solidarity, they can change society. But it all starts with you. You have to be courageous. The rest all follows from that.

Courage is inseparable from justice. It is the determination to do what's right, to build a just society, and to follow the correct path as a human being. It is doing good, taking positive actions, not only for ourselves but for humanity and the world as well. To do this, we need the indispensable power of courage. Our efforts may not call attention to themselves, but in reality, they shine with unsurpassed brilliance.

It takes courage to put a stop to bullying. It takes courage to endure hardships and survive tough circumstances. It takes amazing courage to lead good, productive lives, day after day. And it also takes tremendous courage to share our opinions with our families and friends so that everyone, ourselves included, can move in a more positive direction.

Those with the courage to do what is right, no matter what others say, possess a "precious sword" of limitless power. In Buddhism, such people are called bodhisattvas and Buddhas.

People of genuine courage have no underhanded

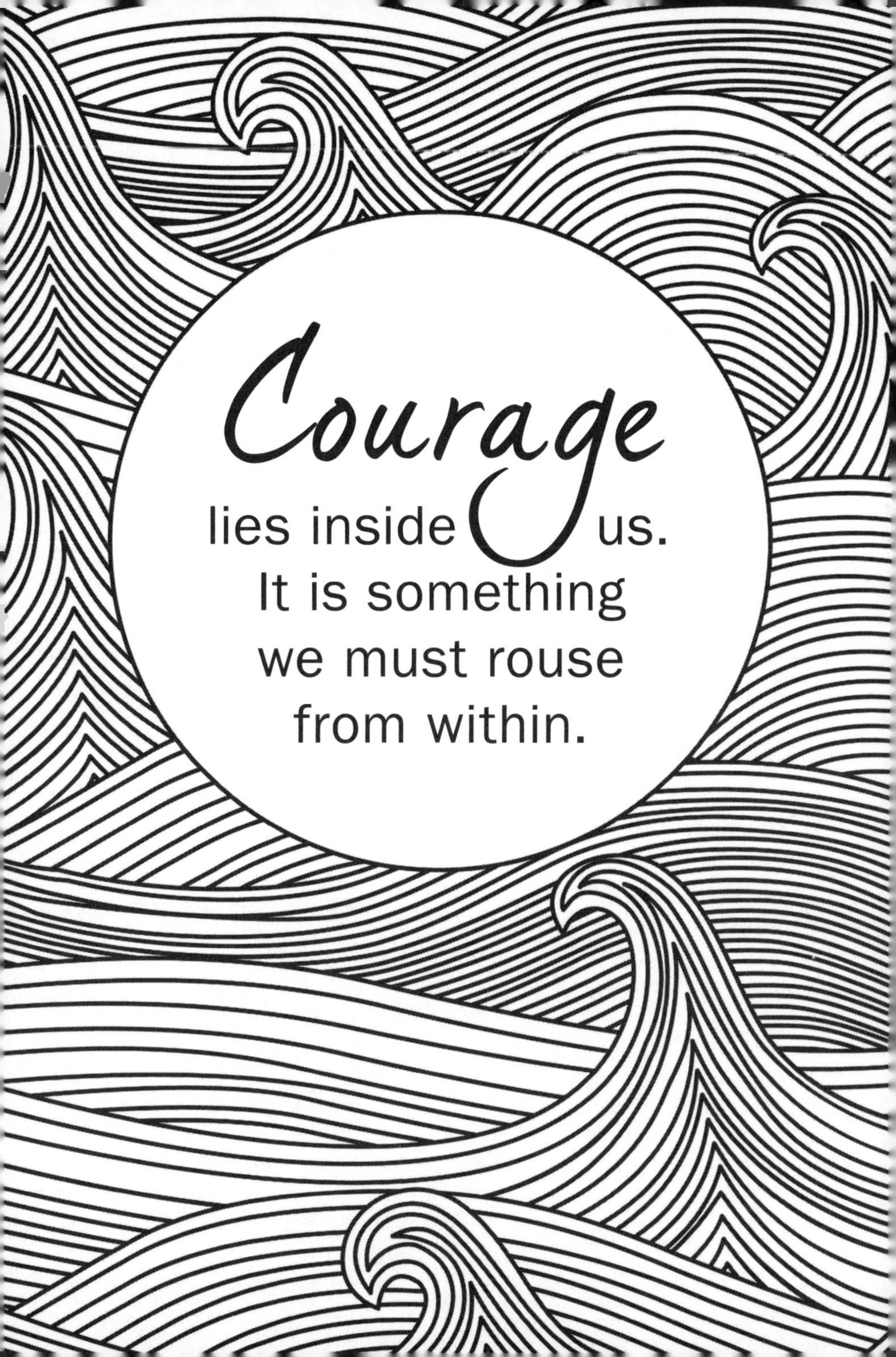
Courage
lies inside us.
It is something
we must rouse
from within.

motivations. They are straightforward and honest—which is why they are often misunderstood and even treated as villains. In contrast, there are others who are skillful manipulators, who scheme and self-promote to gain popularity. Many people are fooled by their apparent success and even envy them. However others may be, those who have done what is right—even if misunderstood, scorned, or harassed as a result—have a clear conscience. They are victors.

True courage is defined by whether it is motivated by justice and compassion. Mr. Toda used to say:

> *It's hard for us ordinary mortals to have compassion. Emotions get in the way, or we just can't be bothered. Though compassion is important, it's difficult for us. But we can have courage. Practically speaking, having courage is our way of acting with compassion.*

And in fact, if we act with courage, we find that our compassion for others actually grows deeper. Courage is indeed the highest virtue.

PERSONAL RELATIONSHIPS

Responding to questions from high school students, President Ikeda discusses friendship and relationships from various perspectives.

Friendship is the most beautiful, powerful, and precious thing in life. It is your greatest treasure. No matter how successful or wealthy a person is, without friends life is sad and lonely. A lack of friends can also lead to a narrow, self-centered existence.

In this vast universe, we have been born together at the same time on this tiny planet. And how rare is it to find, among the 5.8 billion[11] members of the human race, truly caring and honest friends who understand our thoughts and feelings without the need for a lot of words and with whom we can relax and be ourselves.

Even being in the same class at school with someone is the result of a profound connection. Some of you may have found genuine friends among your classmates. If you have, please treasure them. But if you feel you don't have any close friends right now, please don't worry. Just decide that the reason you don't have any now is so you'll be able to make the most wonderful friends later on. Concentrate your energies now on becoming the best person you can. In the future, you might even make friends all around the world.

In any event, friendship is up to you, not the other person. It all depends on you. I hope you will be loyal and true friends, not fair-weather friends who are there when all is well but disappear when something bad happens.

And when you graduate from school, I hope you will have grown to be generous, warmhearted people who can say to your friends with all honesty: "I will never forget you. If you ever have a problem or something you want to talk about, don't hesitate to come to me. And I hope I can go to you too."

—*What kind of advice would you give someone who feels that a friend has suddenly started to treat them coldly but has no idea why?*

I think the best thing to do at such times is gather your courage and ask what's wrong. In many cases, you'll probably be surprised to find that what you imagined wasn't your friend's intention at all. Quite often, when you distance yourself from a friend because you're too afraid to ask what's wrong, the other person may in fact also be feeling hurt and lonely.

Human relationships are like a mirror. Often when you are thinking "If my friend were only a bit nicer to me, I'd be more open with her," your friend may well be thinking "If only she were more open with me, I'd be nicer to her." That's why it's important to be the one who starts the conversation. If you still get a cold response, then you know that the problem lies with your friend, not with you.

Sometimes, there's nothing we can do about the way others feel. People's hearts change. What do you do when that happens? Adopt the attitude "Though others may change, I never will." If you are treated coldly or someone lets you down, resolve not to do the same to others. Those who betray others' trust only hurt themselves, as if they are driving a spike into their own hearts, without even being aware of it.

Shakyamuni is described as a person who always made the effort to reach out and speak to others—something that you need to be strong in order to do.

There may be times in life when others let you down or disappoint you. Nichiren Daishonin was betrayed by many of his followers, even though he was the Buddha of the Latter Day of the Law. I've had people turn against me, too, people for whom I'd done a great deal. But I was never in the least surprised; rather, it's something I accept as a fact of life.

At such times, you need to be brave. You haven't done anything wrong, so just go on living with self-confidence and assurance. Those who betray or bully others are in the wrong. They are to be pitied.

If a friend betrays your trust, just forge new friendships. Don't lose your trust in everyone just because someone has hurt you. If you don't trust anyone you may avoid being hurt or disappointed, but you'll become a closed, narrow person. In truth, those who have suffered deeply are able to be kinder to others. You have to be strong.

Be like the sun. Not all of the light of the sun falls on planets that will reflect it back. The sun's rays also spread out into empty space, seemingly wasted. Yet, the sun still goes on shining brightly. You may find that those who reject the radiant light of your friendship will naturally fade out of your lives. But the more you shine your light, the more brilliant your own lives will become. Follow the path that you believe in, no matter what others think or do. If you remain constant and stay true to yourselves, others will definitely one day come to understand your sincere intent.

You are also fortunate in that you can chant Nam-myoho-renge-kyo. I know of many people who suffered from bullying, but when they challenged their situations through earnestly chanting Nam-myoho-renge-kyo, they suddenly found one day that the bullying had stopped. Through chanting Nam-myoho-renge-kyo when you are suffering, you can quite naturally overcome that suffering, almost without being aware of it. Often it's only when you look back that you realize it.

I hope you will also chant for your friends. That is the greatest expression of friendship. You may have friends who are sick, who cannot attend school, or are struggling to cope with problems at home. Whatever the case may be, the best thing you can do is to chant for them. Your prayers, like radio waves, though invisible, will definitely reach them.

Follow the path that YOU believe in, no matter what others think or do.

It is also important to chant for those you don't like, find hard to get along with, or feel resentful toward. It may be difficult and perhaps even impossible for you to do so at first. But if you keep trying and chant for them, the situation will change. Perhaps you will change, or they will change. Either way, the situation will move in a more positive direction. Many people have experienced this firsthand. Above all, becoming a person who is able to chant for the happiness of such challenging individuals will be your greatest fortune.

The influence of friends is sometimes stronger than that of parents or anyone else. If you have good friends, friends who are trying to improve and develop themselves, you'll improve and grow too. Andrew Carnegie (1835–1919), the American steel magnate, modestly attributed his success to having gathered around him people who were far more talented and capable than he. This was his philosophy of life. The only way to make good friends is to be a good friend yourself. Good people gather around other good people.

I hope you will be accepting and supportive of others. Please become people with hearts as broad as a great river, as wide as the ocean, as vast as the blue sky. Wonderful friendships will unfold from such big hearts.

LOVE AS A SOURCE OF GROWTH

President Ikeda explains that the ideal love relationship is one where both parties inspire each other to realize vibrant growth and develop as human beings.

Just as naturally as spring brings flowers and winter brings snow, youth is a time of awakening to feelings of love and attraction. This is one of the stages of life. You are entering a new period in your life, just as the sun marks a new day by rising brightly at dawn.

Everyone's concerns about love and relationships are different. It depends on your personality, your situation, and your environment. There is no one single approach that will solve everyone's problems. In addition, everyone is perfectly free to fall in love or be attracted to someone. Who you decide to go out with or have a relationship with is your own choice, and it's not really anyone else's business.

The only advice I would like to give you on this subject, as an older friend, is not to let your relationship make you lose sight of pursuing your all-important personal development.

The purpose of your studies and after-school activities, such as team sports and clubs, is to build a foundation for your life, to make you a strong person. Worries about your personality and your relations with friends are also nutrients for building a strong self.

The same is true of love. Love should help you grow as a person; it should invigorate you and help you realize your full potential. This is the basic premise. But as the saying "Love is blind" suggests, when people are in love they often lose the ability to see themselves objectively.

If you allow your new relationship to worry your parents, to lead you into bad behavior, or to stop you from studying, then you and your partner are acting as negative influences on, or hindrances to, each other. Neither of you will be happy if you just end up hurting each other.

The question is: Does the person you like inspire you to work harder at your studies or distract you from them? Does that person's presence make you more determined to devote greater energies to after-school activities, be a better friend, a more thoughtful son or daughter? Does this person inspire you to realize your future goals and work to achieve them? Or is that person your central focus, overshadowing all else, including your after-school activities, your friends and family, and even your goals for the future?

It's not good for either of you if your relationship causes you both to forget what you should be doing now, to forget your goals and dreams. A healthy relationship is one in which two people encourage each other to reach their respective goals while sharing each other's hopes and dreams. A relationship should be a source of inspiration, invigoration, and hope to live your lives to the fullest.

Dante Alighieri (1265–1321) is one of the greatest poets who ever lived. His great love, Beatrice, was his inspiration

LOVE

should be the driving force for living with strength and courage.

in life. He loved her from the time he was a boy, and then happened to meet her again by chance when he was eighteen. He wrote of the deep emotion he felt on that occasion in his *Vita Nuova* (*The New Life*). As Dante struggled to find a way to express his feelings for Beatrice, he invented a new poetic form in *The Divine Comedy,* his lifework. Beatrice opened the door of artistic creation for him.

But his love for Beatrice would never be requited. She married another man and died young. Yet Dante kept loving her. His love forged, elevated, and deepened his spirit into something more lofty and noble. In *The Divine Comedy,* Beatrice is depicted as a gentle, benevolent being who guides him to heaven.

Of course, Dante lived in a different age and perhaps a different country from you. But I think there are many things to be learned from this great poet who stayed true to his own feelings, whether they were reciprocated or not, and transformed them into his guiding inspiration in life. I truly believe that love should be a positive impetus for our lives, the driving force for living with strength and courage.

"LEARNING IS LIGHT, IGNORANCE IS DARKNESS"

Those who keep learning throughout life remain youthful. President Ikeda discusses the importance of cultivating the habit of learning while we are young.

There is a Russian saying: "Learning is light, ignorance is darkness." Of course, "learning" here does not refer only to studying at a university. In a broader sense, learning is self-improvement, while ignorance is stagnation. The spirit of learning leads to peace, progress, and prosperity, while ignorance leads to misery, misfortune, and impoverishment.

In my youth, I studied while working. Around 1950, Mr. Toda's businesses were in serious trouble. It was the most difficult time for me, as I was also in poor health. Yet I never felt unhappy. Spending my days working alongside the person I had chosen as my mentor, I hadn't the slightest regret. My only frustration was that I couldn't study as much as I wanted to.

As if he knew my thoughts, Mr. Toda said to me: "Don't worry. I will teach you everything you would learn at a university. Just be patient. Leave your education to me."

Those who continue learning, who stay active and engaged, remain forever

YOUNG.

From that time, I spent every Sunday at Mr. Toda's home, receiving private instruction from him. With his wide-ranging scholarship, which encompassed government, economics, literature, physics, astronomy, and other fields of science, he became a perfect tutor, imparting to me all of the knowledge he had acquired in his lifetime.

Eventually, in addition to Sundays, the classes expanded to weekday mornings before work. Mr. Toda's classes were extremely demanding. Through this training by my mentor in the midst of our arduous struggles, I built the foundation for my life.

Mr. Toda was always studying. Two weeks before he died, he sternly asked me what I had been reading, adding: "Never forget to keep reading. I'm presently up to volume three of the [ancient Chinese classic] *Compendium of Eighteen Histories.*" At that time, he was extremely weak, to the extent that he could no longer stand or walk unaided. The intense resonance of his voice, however, still reverberates in my ears.

Those who continue learning, who stay active and engaged, remain forever young. Lives that continue improving are like the water of a ceaselessly flowing river, always fresh and pure.

Of the many people I have met, it was the eminent British historian Arnold J. Toynbee (1889–1975) who impressed me most deeply with his unwavering devotion to learning.

After repeated invitations from Professor Toynbee, I had the opportunity to meet and engage in discussion with him for a total of forty hours over ten days in 1972 and 1973. The content of our dialogue was published in 1975. Since then it has been translated into English under the title of *Choose Life*, as well as into French, German, and many other languages, and has been well received around the world. I am delighted at the result, hoping it might repay in some small way the sincerity of Professor Toynbee, who took the time to engage in those lengthy discussions with me, someone many years his junior.

The year after our dialogue ended, Professor Toynbee was incapacitated by illness. Unfortunately, the outlook for his recovery was not good, and it appears that he never fully regained his faculties. In a letter I received from his wife, Veronica, she wrote that even in that condition her husband asked for books, and although it was doubtful that he could actually read, he turned the pages as if he could.

I was deeply moved to read this. Even when illness deprived him of his full awareness, Professor Toynbee's dedicated efforts in scholarly research had become an expression of his life itself, always aiming higher and seeking to learn. I felt he was the model of a great individual who fully deserved the recognition he had gained as one of the leading thinkers of the twentieth century.

It is easy to pay lip service to lifelong learning. With Japan's emergence as an economic superpower, its people have more free time. They engage in a wide range of hobbies. But simply having the time and attending classes somewhere won't guarantee inner enrichment. The key is whether one has a vibrant desire to improve and grow.

Professor Toynbee kept books beside him even when he

was bedridden. Learning had become a habit, a good habit, for him. Those who acquire that habit when they are young are fortunate.

In the workplace and the home, as well as in the events of daily life, we can always find precious opportunities to learn. There are those who use five spare minutes to read a newspaper, open a book, listen to the news, or gain something from an encounter with another person. Though they may seem busy, such people can transform that very busyness into learning. Laziness is the first step toward stagnation. Let us lead lives nourished by the rich wellspring of a desire for self-improvement, maintaining a lively interest and curiosity about everything.

BE SUNS ILLUMINATING A NEW WORLD

President Ikeda offers advice to SGI-USA youth division members on life and faith.

Youth is a time full of worries and problems. Young people's hearts are constantly vacillating. You are worried about your future, your personality, relationships, social issues, and life in general. You are confused and anxious. You are troubled by the gap between ideals and reality, and may sometimes fall into self-hatred and become consumed with insecurity and fear.

Youth is a season of emotional turmoil and suffering. This is the reality of youth, no matter what the country. In a certain sense, that's how it should be. You are not the only ones suffering like this, and in this period of change and growth, these feelings probably can't be helped.

The important thing is not to be impatient. You can't attain peace of mind or social stability all at once. It takes time. If a plane tries to take off without taxiing down the runway and gradually building up speed, it won't succeed. And even if it takes off, if it lacks sufficient fuel and good maintenance, it won't stay in the air long. It may even crash.

Life and Buddhist practice are like a marathon. You may

at times run out front and at times fall behind. But what matters is the final moment at the finish line. The training you undergo in your youth is all for that final, true victory. That's why you need to study as hard as you can now. Keep chanting Nam-myoho-renge-kyo and build up a reservoir of life force. Steadily move ahead on the fundamental path of putting your faith into practice in life, in your own distinct way.

The sun rises every day. It never takes a break. If you do the same, persistently pressing ahead in accord with the Mystic Law, the ultimate Law of the universe, you will come to enjoy a wonderful life of complete satisfaction and fulfillment, far surpassing anything you imagined. Please be assured that this is the most certain and valuable way to spend your youth.

We are pioneers embracing this great philosophy, of which so much of humankind is still unaware. It is, therefore, extremely important to demonstrate just how wonderful Nichiren Buddhism truly is by showing actual proof of its benefit in our lives. Seeing such proof will enable people to realize the greatness and originality of this Buddhism and see that it is different from anything they have encountered before.

Nichiren Daishonin writes, "Even more valuable than reason and documentary proof is the proof of actual fact" (WND-1, 599). Of course, you shouldn't overreach yourselves just trying to show proof. All you need do is present an example of steadily seeking to improve and develop yourselves in the way most natural for you—in your daily lives, in your families, your workplaces, your communities, and in your character. Just carry out your human revolution in your own way. In doing so, you will naturally come to impress others with your vitality, hope, conviction, and reassuring presence. That, in itself, will build the foundation for sharing Nichiren Buddhism with others, without any need for words.

There's no need to rush in our efforts to share Buddhism. I feel it's better to be strict and uphold sound standards for membership, rather than just increase our numbers.

✡

All people have a fabulous "new world"—a yet-undiscovered-realm—within them. It is called the world of Buddhahood. But most of humanity is still not aware of its existence. Our Buddhist practice is the effort to fully tap and activate this "new world" of Buddhahood, a realm of infinite power and potential. Once we awaken to the world of Buddhahood within us, our lives are filled with unsurpassed joy. An entirely "new world" also opens up in our lives and in society. Communicating this to others is our mission.

CHERISH HIGH IDEALS

Through the guidance of second Soka Gakkai President Josei Toda, President Ikeda calls on young people to strive with all their might to realize high ideals.

Naturally, there are many different ways to live your youth, and there is no need to suggest a single approach for everyone. But whatever path you choose, what will play a decisive role in the direction your life takes into the future is whether you live the days of your youth to the fullest or let them slip by without making any real effort.

Mr. Toda often gave us guidance to the effect: "If you're going to do something big, it's important that you have the determination to achieve it in your twenties and thirties. If you wait until you're in your forties, and then suddenly decide to embark on some great venture, it becomes that much more difficult to succeed."

He also advised: "Young people should cherish dreams that seem almost too big to accomplish. Inevitably in life, we're only able to achieve a fraction of what we'd like to. So if your dreams are too small to begin with, you'll end up not being able to accomplish anything. What good, then, will you

Young people should cherish dreams that seem almost too big to accomplish.

have created with your life?"

Striving to realize a high ideal in your twenties and thirties is the key to enjoying unsurpassed satisfaction and fulfillment in this seemingly long yet short existence. You're only young once. How unfortunate it would be to reach your forties and fifties and be filled with sadness and regret. A life of discontent—a life unfulfilled and half-realized like a sputtering, smoldering fire that never leaps into bright flames—is also a terrible waste. That's why you should burn your brightest and strive your hardest in your youth when you are at the height of your powers and your health. It is all for your own benefit.

Mr. Toda taught that young people should cherish high ideals and advance with bright, burning energy. The higher the summit you aim for, the greater the satisfaction you will savor when you reach the peak. This is a way of life filled with passion and growth, brimming with the limitless power of faith in the Mystic Law.

Kosen-rufu is the supreme summit for humankind, the most meaningful and noble ideal. It is also the most realistic ideal, and one that is most urgently needed by society and the times. Dedicate your youth and your life, fully and without reservation, to the great ideal of kosen-rufu. Such a life accords with the teachings of Nichiren Daishonin and embodies the essence of the unchanging Soka Gakkai spirit.

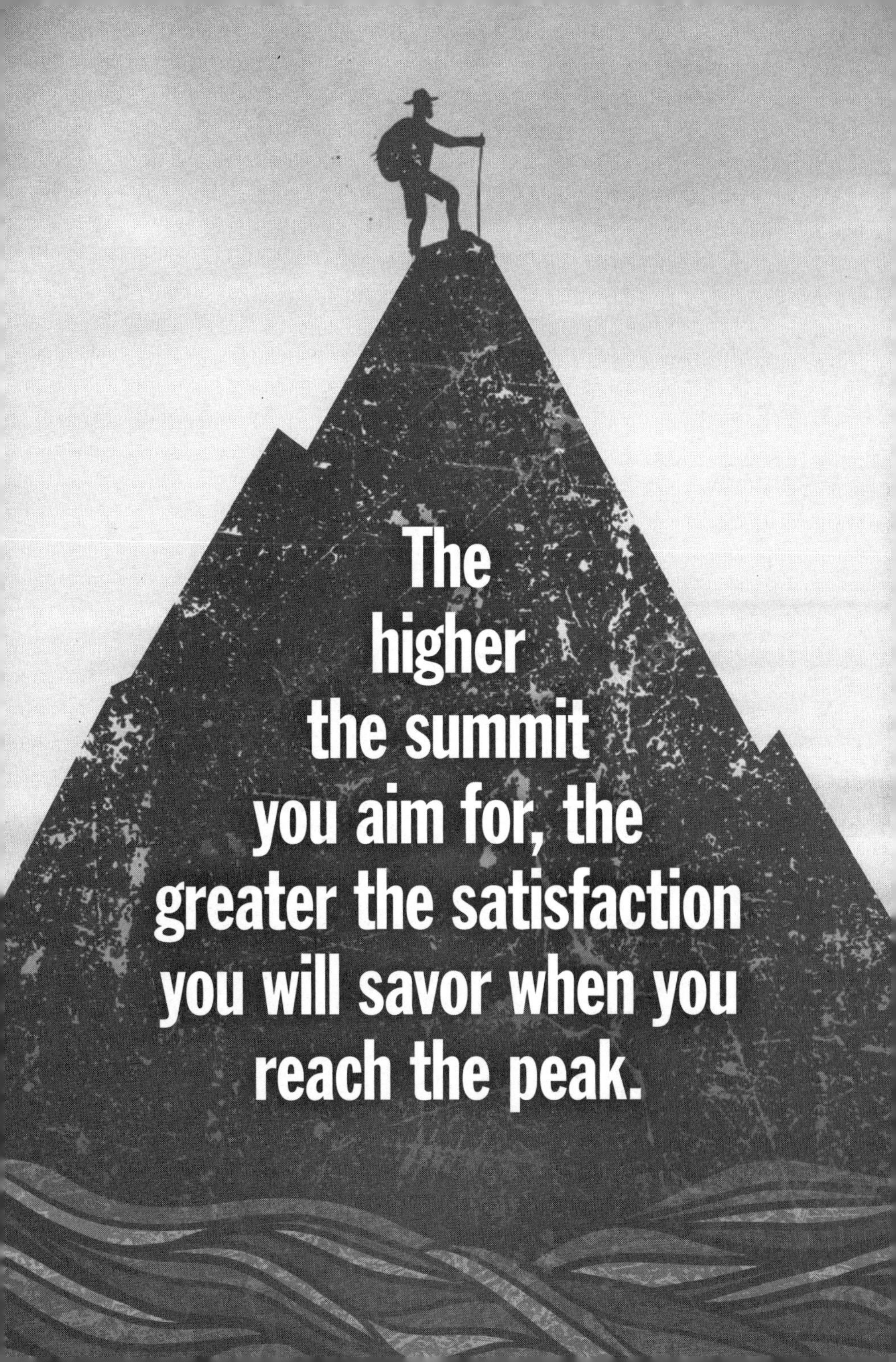
The
higher
the summit
you aim for, the
greater the satisfaction
you will savor when you
reach the peak.

NOTES

1. Translated from German. Carl Hilty, "Glück im unglück" [Happiness Amid Misfortune], *Neue Briefe* (New Letters) (Leipzig: J. C. Hinrichs'sche Buchhandlung, 1906), 57.

2. Translated from German. Carl Hilty, *Für Schlaflose Nächte* [For Sleepless Nights] (Leipzig: J. C. Hinrichs'sche Buchhandlung, 1908), 71.

3. Ibid., 193.

4. Friedrich Nietzsche, *Thus Spoke Zarathustra: A Book for Everyone and No One,* trans. R. J. Hollingdale (London: Penguin Books, 1969), 220.

5. Translated from Japanese. Josei Toda, *Toda Josei zenshu* [The Collected Writings of Josei Toda] (Tokyo: Seikyo Shimbunsha, 1992), 1:158.

6. True cause: Also, mystic principle of the true cause. Nichiren Buddhism directly expounds the true cause for enlightenment as Nam-myoho-renge-kyo, which is the Law of life and the universe. It teaches a way of Buddhist practice of always moving forward from this moment on based on this fundamental Law.

7. Translated from Japanese. Josei Toda, *Toda Josei zenshu* [The Collected Writings of Josei Toda] (Tokyo: Seikyo Shimbunsha, 1991), 1:60.

8. Translated from Japanese. From a lecture on the Lotus Sutra by President Toda to a group of youth division members who were students at Tokyo University, on April 18, 1953.

9. Ibid.

10. See Friedrich von Schiller, *Wilhelm Tell*, trans. and ed. William F. Mainland (Chicago: University of Chicago Press, 1973), 24.

11. The world's population was estimated to be around 5.8 billion in 1996. As of 2017, the figure is 7.5 billion.

REFERENCES

Courage, Conviction, and Hope: Adapted from an essay in a compilation titled *My Thoughts.*

The Problems of Youth Are Themselves Sources of Light: Adapted from an essay in "The Poetry of Light" photo essay series, published in Japanese in the February 27, 2000, *Seikyo Shimbun.*

You Are Each a Precious Individual With a Special Mission: Adapted from *Discussions on Youth.*

Seeking Out Challenges for Self-Development in One's Youth: From the Ninetieth Soka Gakkai Headquarters Leaders Meeting commemorating July 3, held in conjunction with a student division general meeting, Tokyo, June 28, 1995.

Always Look to the Future: From the Chugoku Region Youth Peace General Meeting, Tokyo, May 7, 1995.

Keep Moving Forward: Adapted from *Discussions on Youth.*

Live With an Invincible Spirit: Adapted from *Dialogue of Hope.*

To Young Women's Division Members: A message sent to a Tokyo young women's division chapter leaders meeting, February 9, 2001.

To Appreciate and Care for One's Parents Is the Basis of Genuine Humanity: From a study dialogue series "The Writings of Nichiren Daishonin and the Mentor-Disciple Relationship," volume 3.

Trustworthiness Is the Greatest Asset for Youth: Adapted from an essay in a compilation titled *My Thoughts.*

Our Workplace Is an Important Stage for Our Human Revolution: From the Ninetieth Soka Gakkai Headquarters Leaders Meeting commemorating July 3, held in conjunction with a student division general meeting, Tokyo, June 28, 1995.

Those Who Are Strong Stand Alone: Adapted from *Discussions on Youth.*

Personal Relationships: Adapted from *Discussions on Youth.*

Love as a Source of Growth: Adapted from *Discussions on Youth.*

"Learning Is Light, Ignorance Is Darkness": Adapted from an essay compiled in *Kokoro no shiki* (Seasons of the Heart).

Be Suns Illuminating a New World: From an SGI-USA youth training session, Malibu, California, February 26, 1990.

Cherish High Ideals: From the First Soka Gakkai Headquarters Leaders Meeting, Tokyo, January 20, 1988.